Y0-EKT-048

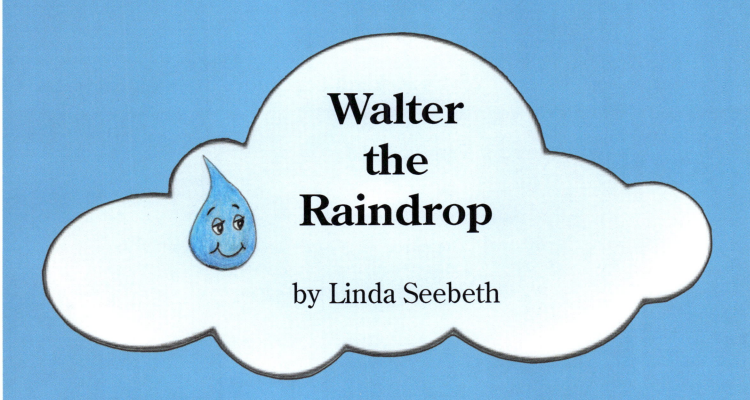

Walter the Raindrop

by Linda Seebeth

With Love and Gratitude for water

 Sustainer of Life

 70% of our bodies and the planet

 The only natural substance found in all 3 physical states (solid, liquid, and gas) at temperatures normally occurring on earth

© Linda Seebeth
All Rights Reserved

Walter was a tiny raindrop falling from a gray cloud high in the sky.

"Wow!" thought Walter, as he gazed down at the fast approaching earth.
"There are some really big things in this world."
He saw vast fields, large buildings, and magnificent tall trees.

"But I'm not big," he sighed.
"I am very small."

As he fell closer to land, Walter was fascinated by bright clusters of
flowers scattered here and there.
"There are many beautiful colors in this world," he marveled.
"How spectacular!"

Then Walter realized, "I am not colorful.

I must not be spectacular."

Nearing the ground, Walter noticed many little critters scurrying about—jumping and flying and crawling.

"They are so busy," Walter thought. "They have a great deal to do.

But I am not busy like them."

Falling toward a corn field, Walter thought, "I'm not big. I'm not colorful. And I'm not busy."

Just as he was beginning to feel like an insignificant drip, Walter heard a voice.

"Why so glum, chum?"

Walter listened as the raindrop explained,
"It's most important to be what you are and do what you do!

I've dropped in before, and believe me, you may be a tiny raindrop, but you're much more than you think!"

As the raindrop swooshed by, Walter suddenly landed on something soft.
The stalk of corn bounced and exclaimed, "Oh joy!
I was so thirsty!
This shower is so refreshing!"

Walter was surprised to receive such a grateful greeting.

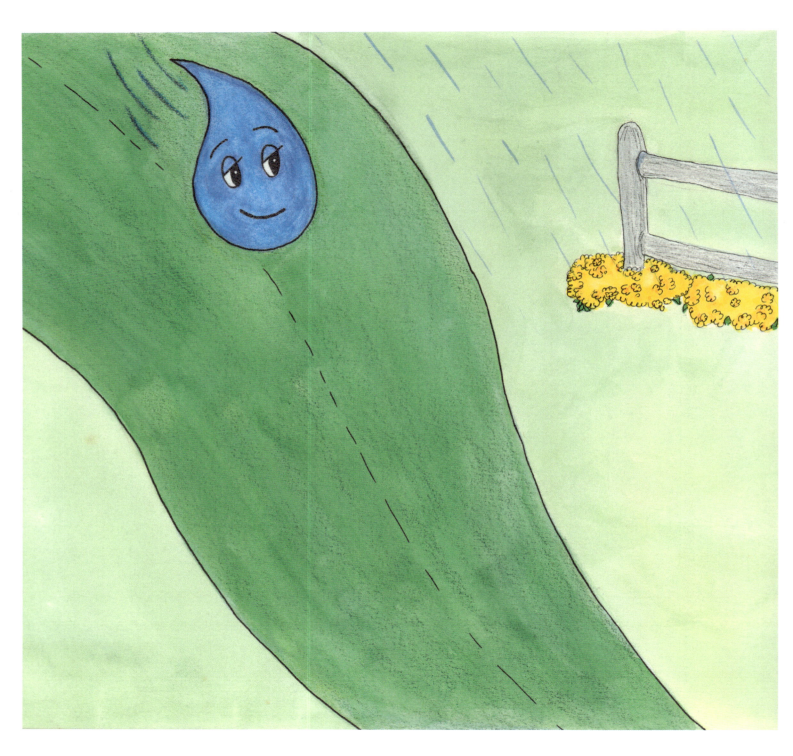

When Walter heard voices singing about the wonderful rain, he looked over
     and saw a farmer and his wife dancing with glee.
"Thank heaven for this rain! I love it! And I love you!" the farmer sang to his wife.
               They both laughed and twirled in delight.

Walter was overjoyed to feel loved and appreciated.
          "I might be a tad important," he pondered.
Swelling up with a feeling of pride caused Walter to roll down the stalk of corn.

Whoosh!
The next thing Walter knew, he had joined together
with many other droplets to become a puddle.

"It feels so good to quench my thirst and
      wash my dusty feathers!" chirped the robin.

Walter smiled as he watched the bird splash and bathe in the puddle.
            He was filled with happiness.

Flowing along the edge of the field, the puddle
   spilled into other puddles and became a stream.
Walter heard ducks quacking their appreciation
      for the fresh rain water.
He saw many animals come to the stream to drink.
Walter was thrilled with the wonder and beauty of it all!

The stream grew wider and deeper,
soon merging with a large river.
Passing through mountain gorges and
wide plains, winding this way and that,
Walter rushed along with the
powerful flow. He knew he
was only a tiny droplet,
yet at the same time,
Walter was a mighty river.

He felt a new sense of
greatness and joy.

When Walter thought he was all that he could possibly be,
   he was amazed to discover that the river opened into a huge body of water.

He had become an ocean— a boundless life-sustaining sea.

One day, Walter was lying on top of an ocean wave, soaking up the warm sunlight, feeling content and thinking about how fantastic the miracle of life could be...

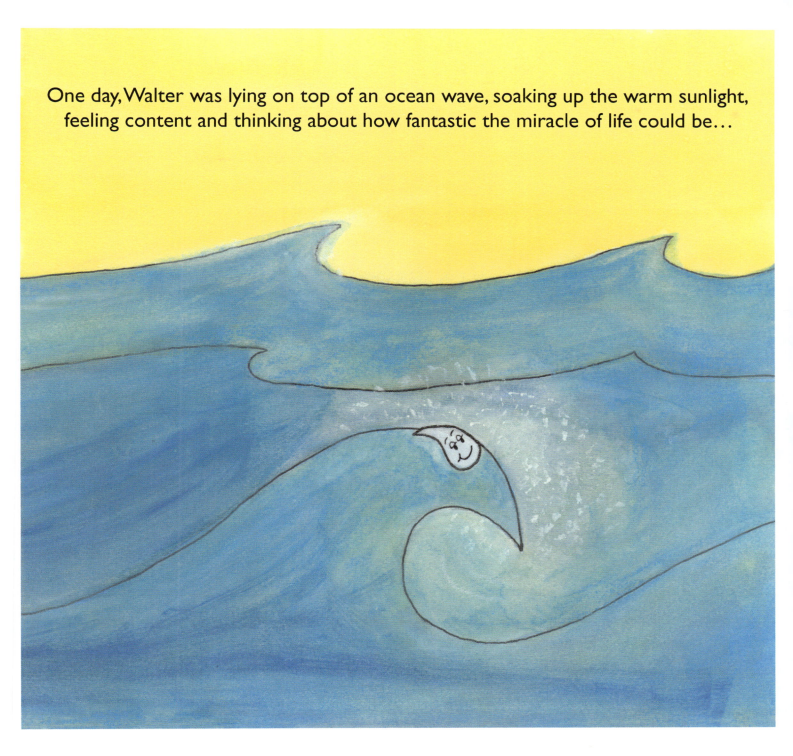

when in a flash, Walter was evaporated up to the air.
Traveling high above the ocean currents,
he looked down in awe at the place he called home.

Time passed and Walter was again dropped out of a cloud. This time he no longer felt unimportant. Perhaps he wasn't big or colorful or busy running to and fro.

Walter was a tiny raindrop, but he knew he was so much more. Walter was an important member of the water planet—Earth.
And every drop counts.

64819446R10019

Made in the USA
Charleston, SC
09 December 2016